Reader's Guides

SECOND SERIES 12

SCOTTISH HISTORY

by

J. D. MACKIE, C.B.E., M.C., LL.D.

*Professor of Scottish History and Literature
in the University of Glasgow*

T0350303

PUBLISHED FOR
THE NATIONAL BOOK LEAGUE
AT THE UNIVERSITY PRESS
CAMBRIDGE
1956

CAMBRIDGE UNIVERSITY PRESS
Cambridge, New York, Melbourne, Madrid, Cape Town,
Singapore, São Paulo, Delhi, Mexico City

Cambridge University Press
The Edinburgh Building, Cambridge CB2 8RU, UK

Published in the United States of America by Cambridge University Press, New York

www.cambridge.org
Information on this title: www.cambridge.org/9781107622166

First published 1956
Re-issued 2013

A catalogue record for this publication is available from the British Library

ISBN 978-1-107-62216-6 Paperback

CONTENTS

INTRODUCTION

Why has Scotland a history of her own? The answer is easy. Scotland has a nationality of her own, and her people have left their mark all over the five continents and the seven seas.

Look at the place-names. Consider the names of the statesmen, soldiers, explorers, doctors and business-men which loom so large in the history of the Dominions, the Colonies, the United States, indeed of every place where British people have been.

Of course, it is curious that Scotland should have a nationality of her own. Her land consists of the northern part of the island of Great Britain—about three-eighths of the whole—with some groups of adjacent islands. The southern part of the main island is occupied by England and Wales.

There is no marked ethnographical difference between the peoples to the north of the Border and those to the south; in both there is a mixture of Germanic and Celtic blood, with an infusion of Scandinavian blood, and doubtless an element usually described as 'pre-Celtic'. It is true that the proportion of non-Germanic blood is higher in Scotland than in England; that some (though not all) of the Scottish Celts are more akin to the Irish than to the Welsh and the people of western England; and that the pre-Celtic element may survive more strongly in the north than in the south. Nonetheless the racial distinction between Scots and English is not very pronounced, and it has been blurred down the centuries by much inter-marriage. Scots and English, for the most part, use the same speech, and Gaelic, though the Scots are very proud of it, is less of a live language than Welsh.

Moreover the general development of Scotland and England has been very much the same. In both countries a primitive population was overrun by successive waves of

Celtic-speakers in a process which was still going on about the beginning of the Christian era. Both felt the pressure of the formative hand of Rome. In both the Celtic, or Romano-Celtic, population was partly submerged by Germanic invaders, and on both the virile Scandinavians made a definite impression.

Both felt the influence of the forces which streamed in from the south-east in the days when the Mediterranean was the mother of all civilization—of Christianity, of the feudal system, later of the Renaissance—and in both countries there developed monarchies which were strong enough to overcome a turbulent baronage and to stand forth as true expressions of nationality.

Gradually the two monarchies came together. Accident of dynasty made the King of Scots, in 1603, King of England too; a community of interests produced the Union of Parliaments in 1707; and although each country by the terms of the Act of Union retained its own church and its own legal system, they have, in spite of some bickering, steadily grown closer together during the last two-hundred-and-fifty years.

Intermarriage, mutual exchange of population—and far more English people come to Scotland now than is generally realised—common business interests, common service to the crown and common share in a great imperial heritage, are gradually wearing away the old antipathies. Scottish nationality is gradually blending into British nationality or even into Commonwealth nationality; but for all that Scotland is Scotland still as England is England.

Why should this be? Why should Scottish nationality be different from that of England? The answer appears if we consider what is this nationality? Nationality is not the same thing as race; English and Scots both are composed of several races. It does not depend on geographical contiguity; for centuries the Jews had no national home; yet Jewish nation-

6

ality was a real thing. It does not lie in the acceptance of a common religion; there are many different forms of religion in Scotland today.

Common race, common speech, common religion and culture, common economic and social conditions, residence in a common homeland, all these things certainly do go to the making of a common nationality. Yet none of them is in itself nationality. Nationality is the result of a common experience of a fairly large group of people over a very long period of time. It is intimately bound up with a history of the people, and it is when we compare the history of Scotland with that of England, that we get the answer to our question. For although the growth of Scotland down the ages resembles in its broad outline that of England, there are nevertheless differences between the two developments, and it is in these differences that the secret of the divergent nationalities is found.

The root of these differences lies in geography. For centuries the island of Great Britain lay upon the fringe of European civilization; it was flat and fertile in the south-east, rugged and hilly in the north-west. Hence it came that the various streams of population and of culture which flowed from the continent established themselves with ease in the south-east, driving before them, in some cases, the less developed populations which they found in occupation. It is quite true that the land now called Scotland received in historic times reinforcements of population which did not come up from the south. From Ireland she received an active Christianity; from the Scandinavian countries a stream of invaders who, though at first they were cruel marauders and later dangerous conquerors, remained at last to contribute a virile element to the native stock.

Nonetheless there remains the essential fact that to some extent new peoples and, to a very large extent, new forms of culture came into Scotland from Europe and through the land which is now called England. The history of Scotland for centuries is a repetition of the same process.

Upon the primitive stocks of bronze-users there may have come some early iron-users direct across the North Sea; but the developed iron culture called la Tène, definitely associated with a Celtic people, came through England.

It was in England that the Romans established an organised province; it was in the fertile lands of the south and east that the Germanic invaders made their main assault. It was in the south-east that the Mediterranean influence again asserted itself with the church and the organised force of the feudal system. At the end of the middle ages the stirring of the Renaissance was felt earlier and more strongly in the south than in the north.

The political results of this long process can readily be discerned. The English kingdom was larger, wealthier, stronger and better organised than that which arose in Scotland. And throughout the centuries it made, with varying degrees of intensity, efforts to overrun or absorb its weaker neighbour to the north.

Sometimes, as in the days of Edward I, Edward III and Oliver Cromwell, England nearly succeeded in her ambition; even in the days of Henry VIII she tried hard to realise her claim of suzerainty. Yet somehow Scotland contrived to maintain her independence, and when she entered into full partnership with England it was as a sister and not as a bondwoman.

Her survival as a free nation was due in part to geography; the rugged land of the north was difficult to approach and, though there may be an element of 'sour grapes' in the English attitude, hardly worth a great effort at conquest. It was due partly to England's pre-occupation with the necessity of dealing with the Scandinavians and later with her desire of making conquests in France. Yet it was due also to Scotland's sense of her own being and dignity, reflected in the long genealogies which take the descent of her kings back to Noah. At all events Scotland was able, if sometimes only just able, to repel the attacks from the south; and in the very act of repelling them her nationality became an articulate thing. Scotland was born fighting.

The nation which emerged differed from England in various ways. In the first place the central power was long in asserting its authority. There remained a radical division between the Gaelic-speaking Highlands and the Lowlands, where Anglo-Norman influences of every kind—religious, governmental, linguistic and architectural—steadily infiltrated. Again, even in the south, the crown had difficulty in controlling its baronage, and the 'New Monarchy' which emerged in the reign of James IV (1488-1513) was not the well-organised machine of the Tudors. Yet again, while it is true that, owing in part to the eternal struggle with England, Scotland lagged behind in cultural development, it is true also that Scotland received something direct from France. The 'Auld Alliance' was primarily political, but it had other sides as well. Scottish churchmen were in touch with France; from France, Scotland got her university system, some of her architecture, some of her literature and some of her speech. It may be added that, through the church, she got some of her law from Rome.

The differences between the kingdoms were accentuated by the Reformation. Generalities are dangerous; but, broadly speaking, in England a strong king allied with a competent 'third estate' against the old church and the old nobility; while in Scotland it was the nobles and the 'third estate' who attacked the old church, and the crown which tried to defend it. In the issue the King of England emerged as head of a Protestant Episcopal church while in Scotland the Kirk, which in the course of its struggles became Presbyterian, tended always to oppose the crown. It is true that James VI had established the royal control in very large measure before he ascended the throne in 1603, but Presbyterian opposition still remained.

The 'Union of the Crowns', though of great significance did not produce at once a common British nationality; it did not even 'open a new chapter in the history of Scotland', but rather gave a new direction to old tendencies. At first the crown, strong in a new prestige and power, established better order and endeavoured to refashion the Scottish church upon the English model; but it overplayed its hand and Charles I was confronted with opposition against an authority disliked partly as being dictatorial and partly as being English. In Scotland began the attack which culminated in the death of Charles. Yet Scotland could not join hands with the triumphant revolutionaries of England; she had no love for Cromwell because she was still Royalist and still Presbyterian, while he was a regicide sectarian.

It is true that Cromwell gave good order, good justice and a measure of toleration. But he remained a great Englishman, and though he endeavoured to unite England and Scotland under a single parliament, the arrangements he proposed were such that, as Robert Blair remarked, 'as for the embodying of Scotland with England, it will be as when the poor bird is embodied into the hawk that has eaten it up'.

In Scotland the Restoration of 1660 was generally welcomed, but it soon appeared that the restored monarchy was more authoritarian than ever, and Scotland joined with England to extrude James VII and II. When after this 'Glorious Revolution' some kind of parliamentary authority was established in both countries it soon became apparent that a mere Union of Crowns would not do; for king and parliament in Scotland might decide one thing and king and parliament in England the exact opposite—witness the disastrous 'Darien Scheme'. Either each country must go its own way or the two parliaments must be united.

So in 1707 the parliaments were united. Since then, the two countries have grown closer together, and although the harmony is not always perfect, each realises that the union is advantageous to both. Scotland still keeps her own kirk and her own law, and in spite of constitutional union, to a marked degree her own nationality.

That is a good thing. For nationality is a precious thing. It is a dear-bought experience. It is, in fact, indestructible; and the union of the kingdoms has been a success only because each side has contributed to the common stock something of its ancestral virtue.

READING LIST

It is impossible to include all the printed material for Scottish history in any list of books; for many of the most important sources are to be found in Government publications—Calendars, Registers, etc.; in the books issued by the great historical clubs; in the Scottish Historical Review, the Proceedings of the Society of Antiquaries of Scotland and other periodicals.

The list here presented is long; and yet it is incomplete; many works worthy of inclusion have perforce been omitted. It may well appear uneven. The explanation is this. Much of the recent work has taken the form of criticism, either expressed or implied, of the recognised canon; some of the old 'standards' have therefore been included along with the new books. Unevenness, too, appears in the content of the different sections. That is because in different periods different factors dominated. At one time, political history seemed to be all important. At other times constitutional and ecclesiastical issues bulked larged in the national history. Recently great attention has been given to social and economic history. These differences are reflected in the lists of books. A very few of the most essential books have been signalised by asterisks.

The following abbreviations have been used:

S.H.S.	..	..	Scottish History Society
S.T.S.	..	..	Scottish Text Society
S.H.R.	..	..	Scottish Historical Review
Hist. Ass.	..	..	Historical Association.

So far as possible dates of the latest editions are given. Prices (net and subject to alteration) are those prevailing in March, 1956, and are given only where a book is known to be available new as this list goes to press.

HISTORICAL APPARATUS

It is impossible to signalise here all the sources available to historians. The following books are of special interest.

BLACK, GEORGE F. comp. *List of Works in the New York Public Library Relating to Scotland*. New York Public Library, 1916.

An immense work, admirably arranged in sections. The best bibliography of Scottish history.

STAIR SOCIETY. *The Sources and Literature of Scots Law*. 1936.

Sections contributed by experts. Very valuable for constitutional history.

MEIKLE, H. W. *A Brief Bibliography of Scottish History*. Hist. Ass. Pamphlet, 1937.

Very convenient.

MACGREGOR, M. B. *The Sources and Literature of Scottish Church History*. John McCallum, 1934.

A slight work, but convenient.

TERRY, C. SANFORD. *A Catalogue of the Publications of Scottish Historical and Kindred Clubs and Societies* continued by Cyril Matheson. 2 vols. Milne & Hutchison, 1928.

An indispensable and extremely efficient index to the works of the great Scottish Clubs in whose publications so much of Scottish history is preserved.

THOMSON, J. MAITLAND. *The Public Records of Scotland*. MacLehose, Jackson, 1922.

A brief, lucid presentation, by a master of his craft who was modest and humane, of a subject which might have been very dull.

DUNBAR, A. H. *The Scottish Kings* 1005–1625. 2nd edn. David Douglas, 1906.

Brief but well authenticated notes upon every reign. Very useful and reliable.

PAUL, Sir JAMES BALFOUR. *The Scots Peerage*. 9 vols. David Douglas, Edinburgh, 1904–1914.

The work of a Lyon King. Extremely important for a history in which the great families played so great a part.

STUART, MARGARET and PAUL, Sir JAMES BALFOUR. *Scottish Family History*. Oliver & Boyd, 1929. 24s.

A very useful guide to the materials for Scottish family history, and to the manner of using them.

GENERAL HISTORIES

SCOTT, Sir WALTER. *Tales of a Grandfather*, 1829–1830.

Begun as a set of stories for his grandson 'Little Johnny Lockhart'. The first series adheres to the idea of a juvenile book. It accepts romantic tales and suffers from Scott's tendency to regard the Middle Ages as static. The second series is from 1603 to 1707 and is definitely a 'grown-up' book; and the third series, though over-weighted with Jacobitism, contains some valuable pictures of life in eighteenth-century Scotland. Still a very useful book.

*BROWN, P. HUME. *History of Scotland*. 3 vols. C.U.P., best edn. 1911. Each vol. 50*s*. 1. *To the Accession of Mary Stuart;* 2. *To the Revolution of* 1689; 3. *To the Disruption*, 1843.

The work of an accurate, well informed and fair-minded historian who wrote at a time when authors hoped to attain complete detachment. In fact, liberal and Presbyterian in tone. Accepting the Whig doctrine, and assuming that 'representation' was the *palladium*, the author is weak upon the Scottish Parliament, and upon the Scottish constitution as it is now understood. Nonetheless, commended by its tolerant outlook and excellent documentation, it remains perhaps the best of the general histories.

LANG, ANDREW. *History of Scotland*. 4 vols. Blackwood, 1900–1907.

A full history in tone generally critical of the 'Whig Tradition'. The author was something of an advocate as well as a historian, but a fair-minded advocate. Rather weak on constitution but strong on periods and aspects which interested him.

MATHIESON, W. L. *Politics and Religion in Scotland*. 2 vols. J. MacLehose, 1902.

—— *Scotland and the Union*, 1905.

—— *The Awakening of Scotland*, 1910.

—— *The Church and Reform in Scotland*, 1916.

In all, a history of Scotland from 1550 to 1843, with special reference to religion. Marked by 'moderatism' and a general distrust of enthusiasm. Well documented.

MACKENZIE, AGNES MURE. *The Foundations of Scotland.* Macmillan and W. & R. Chambers, 1938.

Part of a series which contains:—
Robert Bruce, King of Scots. A. MacLehose, 1934; Oliver & Boyd, 1956. 18s.
The Rise of the Stuarts. A. MacLehose, 1935.
The Scotland of Queen Mary. A. MacLehose and Macmillan, 1936.
The Passing of the Stuarts. A. MacLehose, 1937.
Scotland in Modern Times. Macmillan and Chambers, 1941.

In all, a lively and well written history from a 'nationalist' point of view. Criticisms of the 'English' approach to Scottish questions are not unjustifiable; but the books are marred by obvious antipathy to the English and to Presbyterians.

TERRY, CHARLES SANFORD. *A History of Scotland.* C.U.P., 1920.

A generous history of Scotland by an Englishman. Extremely useful for its genealogical tables.

RAIT, Sir ROBERT. *History of Scotland.* O.U.P. (Home University Library), 1929.

Brief but very good. The author, who wrote much on Scottish history, here arranged his matter topically.

*RAIT, Sir ROBERT and PRYDE, GEORGE S. *Scotland.* Benn, 2nd edn. 1954. 25s.

The only text-book which brings the history of Scotland down to the present day. Much the best thing for Scotland after 1707.

FYFE, J. G. *Scottish Diaries and Memoirs.* 2 vols. Aeneas Mackay, 1928 and 1942.

The extracts with their annotations cover a period from 1550 to 1843. The second volume contains a useful appendix on the subdivisions and re-unitings of the various sections of the Presbyterian Church.

*DICKINSON, W. CROFT, DONALDSON, GORDON and MILNE, ISOBEL, ed. *A Source Book of Scottish History.* Nelson, Vol. 1, 1952; Vol. 2, 1953; each 10s.; Vol. 3 (by Dickinson and Donaldson only) 1954, 21s.

An admirable collection of documents explained by extremely

good notes and constituting the best general history of Scotland up to the year 1707.

MACKIE, R. L. *A Short History of Scotland.* O.U.P., 1931. 15*s.*
A competent and extremely well-written narrative.

MACPHAIL, I. M. M. *A History of Scotland: Book* 1—*To* 1747. *Book* 2—*From* 1702 *to the Present Day.* Edward Arnold. *Book* 1, 1954, 7*s.* 6*d.*; *Book* 2, 1956, 9*s.* 6*d.*
A school book and a very good one. Takes full account of most recent researches.

NOTESTEIN, WALLACE. *The Scot in History.* Cape, 1947.
An estimate, by an American historian of Scottish descent, of the interaction of the Scottish character and the national history.

PREHISTORY

CHILDE, V. GORDON. *The Prehistory of Scotland.* Routledge, 1935.
A valuable book. Scotland has had some great archaeologists of an earlier date, but in this book Professor Childe, with great courage, endeavoured to relate archaeology to history, associating various cultures with definite folks. With it may well be read his pamphlet *Prehistoric Scotland* (Hist. Ass. Pamphlet No. 115, 1940), which contains an extremely useful time-scale, advanced with the necessary *caveats*, but in its main line generally accepted.

—— *Scotland before the Scots.* Methuen, 1946.
This book represents the Rhind Lectures of 1944 delivered before the Society of Antiquaries of Scotland under the title 'The Development of Tribal Society in Scotland in Pre-Roman Times'. In an endeavour to use the methods of the Soviet historians the author tends to emphasise the importance of the community rather than of the individual. In valuable appendices various cultural remains (chambered-cairns, beakers, food-vessels, etc.) are classified typologically, and there are succinct discussions of several important topics.

SCOTLAND IN ROMAN TIMES

Much of the recent work in Scotland is contained in articles in the *Proceedings of the Society of Antiquaries of Scotland* and the *Journal of Roman Studies* and in chapters in the *Cambridge Ancient History*, and the *Oxford History of England*. Good scholars hold different opinions as to the extent and depth of the Roman penetration, but the following books are valuable.

MACDONALD, Sir GEORGE. *The Roman Wall in Scotland.* 2nd edn. O.U.P., 1934. 48*s.*

This represents the life-work of a scholar who was himself responsible for most of the field-work on which his book was based. He knew the Wall personally from end to end and advanced a definite theory as to its construction. His belief that the Wall was abandoned deliberately in 185 has been challenged by recent scholarship but his book, which contains more than one valuable *excursus* on Roman organisation and Roman methods, still remains a standard.

CURLE, J. *A Roman Frontier Post and its People.* J. MacLehose, 1911.

This very handsome book is a monument of the first great scientific investigation of a Roman fort in Scotland. As the author indulged in no uncertain theories, but described, with the aid of magnificent illustrations, the things he actually found, his work has permanent value.

MILLER, S. N., ed. *The Roman Occupation of South-Western Scotland.* Glasgow Archaeological Society, 1952.

This is a series of reports by good scholars of excavations made under the auspices of the Glasgow Archaeological Society. It does not take account of the valuable discoveries made under other auspices in the South West of Scotland, but it is very important as presenting new evidence as to the Roman approach to the western end of the Wall, and as to its maintenance.

RICHMOND, I. A. *Roman Britain* (Pelican History of England). Penguin, 1955. 2*s.* 6*d.*

This is the work of a scholar who has done much excavation in Scotland and the north of England. It contains a map of the Antonine Wall and of the recently discovered fortresses which support its left flank. It represents the best modern opinion upon the influence of the Romans in Britain, and is supplied with an excellent bibliography.

BURN, A. R. *Agricola· and Roman Britain* (Teach Yourself History). English U.P., 1953. 7s. 6d.

This is the work of a classical scholar who has had experience of excavation in Cyprus and elsewhere. He has clothed his narrative with life, but sometimes does not make quite clear where evidence ends and speculation begins.

THE DARK AGES

The relations of the Picts, Scots and Britons one to another are still debated with the enthusiasm shown long ago by Scott's 'Antiquary'. Linguistic, historical, and literary evidences are all involved. Some of the books included in this section are valuable for early mediaeval history.

SKENE, W. F. *Celtic Scotland*. 3 vols. David Douglas, 1886–1890.

The old standard and still valuable.

WATSON, W. J. *History of the Celtic Place-Names of Scotland*.2nd edn. Blackwood, 1926. 30s.

This is the accepted standard on early Scottish philology; and for a period in which much of the available evidence is philological it is extremely valuable for the history of the process by which the Picts, Scots, Britons and Angles coalesced into a single kingdom. The author held that the speech of the original Celtic inhabitants of Britain was a form of P-Celtic; that Q-Celtic was an off-shoot of that speech which appeared first in Ireland. He believed that the princely houses of the Lowlands preserved something of the Roman tradition after the Romans had gone.

JACKSON, K. *Language and History in Early Britain.* University Publications (Language and Literature 4), Edinburgh, 1953. 80s.

A Celtic philologist has written a book in which history and philology are correlated to the better understanding of both. He discusses the nature of possible Roman survivals; the relations of Strathclyde with Rheged and Cumbria; the impact of Germanic conquerors and settlers upon a population in the

Lowlands which was akin in the main to the Celtic population in England and used the same 'Brittonic' speech, perhaps with dialectical differences.

CHADWICK, H. M. *Early Scotland: The Picts,' the Scots and the Welsh of Southern Scotland.* C.U.P., 1949. 30s.

This is the work of a Germanic philologist who died before it was published, and it lacks his final revision. Reverting to the older opinion, he held that the early Bronze-using Celtic invaders spoke a form of Q-Celtic. He equated some of the British tribes of England with those known to Ptolemy as being in Scotland; among which were the Coritani who lived about Leicester. He supposed that their name in the form 'Cruithni', which he identified with Pritani (whence later Britons), was at one time generally applied to most of the early Celtic inhabitants of Britain. The book has been attacked on the grounds of philology and because it rests upon a too great reliance on the old genealogies; but it is of value.

LETHBRIDGE, T. C. *The Painted Men: The Story of the Picts.* Melrose, 1954. 16s.

A gay, vigorous and imaginative book based upon much exploration and excavation on the western coast of Scotland and the Hebrides. The author believes that Picts were invaders from the western coast of Gaul (*Pictavia, Poitou*) where as the *Pictones* they had been allies of Caesar against the Veneti of Brittany. For him the Picts were primarily a sea-people, the builders of the *brochs* and the earth-houses, who established themselves in might over much of Scotland, eventually giving their name to most of the land north of the Firths. They remained, however, a great sea-people and became dread enemies of the Roman province of Britain. Not accepted by most scholars in its entirety, the book has life. It is well illustrated.

WAINWRIGHT, F. T., ed. *The Problem of the Picts.* Nelson, 1955. 21s.

This is a collection of essays founded in the main upon contributions made to one of the Summer Schools which the editor directs. The general effect of the essays is to suggest that much of the Pictish civilisation was derived from the south. The case may have been overstated, but the reputation of the authors demands that their views must be very seriously considered.

19

SIMPSON, W. DOUGLAS. *St. Ninian and the Origins of the Christian Church in Scotland.* Oliver & Boyd, 1940. 10s.

Dr. Simpson is an archaeologist who has written much on early Scottish History. In this book, as in *The Celtic Church in Scotland* (Aberdeen University Press, 1935) and in his other writings, he maintains that Scottish Christianity owes less to Columba and more to Ninian than has been commonly supposed. He regards the Ninianic Mission as part of the assertion of *Romanitas* against *Barbaria* made by Stilicho, and holds that the Ninianic Missionaries penetrated deep into historic Pictland. His views are not universally accepted. See *Transactions of the Dumfriesshire and Galloway Natural History and Antiquarian Society*, 1950: Important.

MEDIAEVAL SCOTLAND

Early Sources of Scottish History, 2 vols. collected and translated by A. O. ANDERSON. Oliver & Boyd, 1923. 70s.

Essential. The work of a scholar who knew the Celtic and the Scandinavian languages as well as Latin. Almost all the information about Scotland available in sources other than English chronicles is presented with the aid of very valuable notes and a great bibliography. The passages are all translated into English.

Scottish Annals from English Chroniclers, ed. A. O. Anderson. David Nutt, 1908.

The passages in the English chronicles relative to Scottish history are printed in English translations with very useful notes. The evidence is clearly presented and allowed to speak for itself.

RITCHIE, R. L. GRAEME. *The Normans in Scotland.* Edinburgh University Press, 1954. 50s.

A valuable account of the influence of the Normans in the development of Scotland from the reign of Malcolm Canmore to the reign of Malcolm IV. Emphasis is laid upon the achievements of the royal house, influenced by English marriages, and inspired by a form of religion which came from the South, though, as the author shows, not always through England. A work which cannot be disregarded.

DOWDEN, JOHN. *The Mediaeval Church in Scotland.* J. MacLehose, 1910.

A well-informed survey, tolerant and wise.

—— *The Bishops of Scotland.* J. MacLehose, 1912.

Being notes on the lives of all the Bishops, under each of the sees, prior to the Reformation. Keith's *Scottish Bishops*, 1734, an excellent book for its time (best edition 1824) is brought up to date. For some corrections, see the *Handbook of British Chronology* published by the Royal Historical Society, 1939, pp. 207–233.

LAWRIE, Sir ARCHIBALD CAMPBELL. *Early Scottish Charters prior to A.D.* 1153. J. MacLehose, 1905.

A courageous attempt to select, from a great mass of charters, some which illustrate best the development of Scottish history. The documents are produced in Latin, but the full notes are in English. Examination shows that the texts are not always entirely accurate, but this is a very handy and useful book.

—— *Annals of the Reigns of Malcolm and William, Kings of Scotland.* J. MacLehose, 1910.

A presentation of Scottish history in extracts from original authorities, usually in the original languages, though the French of Jordan de Fantosme, clerk of Henry of Blois, Bishop of Winchester, is translated. Useful notes, concerned mainly with persons. No attempt at argument.

SIMPSON, W. DOUGLAS, ed. *The Viking Congress.* Oliver & Boyd, 1954. 30s.

A series of papers delivered at a Congress whereat most of the Scandinavian countries were represented. Devoted mainly to Norse influences in the north of Scotland.

BRØGGER, A. W. *Ancient Emigrants.* O.U.P., 1929.

A study of the Scandinavian impact upon Scotland from the earliest times to Haakon's expedition of 1263. Important as giving evidence that the first Scandinavians to come were not sea-raiders, but poor peasants from a bleak part of Norway, in search of a better land. Not all the author's theories have been accepted.

21

FERGUSSON, Sir JAMES, Bt., of Kilkerran *Alexander the Third*. A. MacLehose, 1937.

A small book founded upon good evidence. The author has made a personal study of the scene of the Battle of Largs.

COOPER, Lord. *Supra Crepidam*. Nelson, 1951. 7*s*. 6*d*.

Four illuminating essays, concerned mainly with the mediaeval history of Scotland, by the late Lord Justice-General and Lord President of the Court of Session.

FERGUSSON, Sir JAMES, Bt., of Kilkerran. *William Wallace*. A. MacLehose, 1938.

Small but takes account of nearly all the very limited evidence about the real Wallace. Emphasises that Wallace came of good family, and asserts his claim to be a real leader of the Scottish resistance, countering the views of Barron (*infra*).

MACKENZIE, A. MURE. *Robert Bruce, King of Scots*. A. MacLehose, 1934; Oliver & Boyd, 1956. 18*s*. (See p. 15 *supra*).

A criticism of Sir Herbert Maxwell's *Life of Bruce* (which lays stress on the importance of the Anglo-Norman Lowlands, and is somewhat critical of Bruce's conduct before 1306).

BARBOUR, JOHN. *The Bruce*. 2 vols. Scottish Text Society, 1894.

A sub-contemporary account (*circ.* 1375) in the form of an epic poem written by an author who had been at pains to collect evidence. Note that Blind Harry's *Wallace* (*circ.* 1475) though it has some historical significance, is largely legendary, and unlike Barbour's *Brus* full of hate towards the English.

BARRON, EVAN MACLEOD. *The Scottish War of Independence: A Critical Study*. Nisbet, 1914. 2nd edn. Carruthers, 1934.

This emphasises the importance of the north of Scotland in the struggle for independence and of Sir Andrew de Moray, who fought along with Wallace and was probably mortally wounded at Stirling Bridge.

McKENZIE, W. MACKAY. *The Battle of Bannockburn*. J. MacLehose, 1913.

Advances the theory that the English crossed the Burn on the night before the Battle. For criticisms, see S.H.R. XI, 233 and XXIX, 207.

LATE MEDIAEVAL SCOTLAND

BALFOUR-MELVILLE, E. W. M. *James I, King of Scots*. Methuen, 1936.

An accurate and painstaking account of a most important reign. Founded upon original authorities, and marked by extreme caution, it contains information not easily found elsewhere.

DUNLOP, Dr. ANNIE I. *The Life and Times of James Kennedy, Bishop of St. Andrews*. Oliver & Boyd, 1950. 25s.

Published to commemorate the five-hundredth anniversary of the College of St. Salvator founded by Bishop Kennedy, who was distinguished both as a churchman and as a statesman. Perhaps too adulatory, but a learned and altogether worthy tribute to a great man.

CAMERON, ANNIE I. *The Apostolic Camera and Scottish Benefices, 1418–88*. O.U.P., 1934.

The author, now Dr. Dunlop (see above) has worked much in the Vatican Library. An important study of the development of a situation which contributed to the birth of the Reformation.

HANNAY, R. K. *The Scottish Crown and the Papacy*, 1424–1860. Hist. Ass. Pamphlet, 1931.

Valuable.

THE REFORMATION AND THE SIXTEENTH CENTURY

FLEMING, DAVID HAY. *The Reformation in Scotland*. Hodder & Stoughton, 1910.

A work of great learning, produced by a convinced Presbyterian. To some the opinions may seem extreme, but the facts are irrefutable.

HERKLESS, JOHN and HANNAY, R. K. *The Archbishops of St. Andrews*. Vol. 4. *David Beaton*. Blackwood, 1913.

Difficult to read. No chapters and no index; but factual and founded upon original authority. (See also in the same series Vol. 2, *Andrew Forman;* Vol. 3, *James Beaton* and Vol. 5 *John Hamilton*. Vols. 2 and 5 only of this series are available, each 7s. 6d.)

DICKINSON, Prof. W. CROFT, ed. *John Knox's History of the Reformation in Scotland.* 2 vols. Nelson, 1949. 42*s*.

A version in English to take the place of the edition edited by David Laing (Wodrow Society, 1846–1848). Translation justified by the author on the ground that the MS used by Laing was in fact the work of eight scribes and has no orthographical value. Some of the original documents have been removed to appendices at the end of vol. 2. The introduction, notes, and index are all admirable.

PERCY, Lord EUSTACE. *John Knox.* Hodder & Stoughton, 1937.

A generous appraisal of Knox, whose less-known works are effectively used to illustrate the development of his ideas.

MACGREGOR, JANET S. *The Scottish Presbyterian Polity.* Oliver & Boyd, 1926. 7*s*. 6*d*.

Very valuable, as showing that the Scottish Reformation was not, as has often been supposed, based entirely upon the Genevan model.

FLEMING, D. HAY. *Mary Queen of Scots.* Hodder & Stoughton, 2nd edn., 1898.

A short book with an enormous battery of notes. Unfortunately goes down only to 1568 and a contemplated second volume never appeared. The writer evidently believes in Mary's guilt in the Darnley-Bothwell affair, but this is a just book. Much the best of the many books on Mary, if the notes are read along with the text.

GORE-BROWNE, ROBERT. *Lord Bothwell.* Collins, 1937.

An interpretative biography in the new manner. The writer argues that Bothwell was made the scapegoat of conspirators far more guilty than he, and uses original authorities; but he cannot do more than show that some of Bothwell's accusers were probably themselves guilty. Interesting, but not really as reliable as the old *Life of James Hepburn, Earl of Bothwell* by Frederik Schiern (trans. D. Berry, David Douglas, 1880).

LEE, MAURICE, Jr. *James Stewart, Earl of Moray.* New York, Columbia University Press, 1953 (dist. by O.U.P.). 32*s*.

A well documented biography based upon sound authorities.

In the main a successful defence of Mary's half-brother who has been regarded by some as her evil angel. Not uncritical; but in the manner of some American historians, seems to balance one doubtful character against another in discussing European politics.

WILLSON, DAVID HARRIS. *James VI and I*. Cape, 1956. 30*s*.

An ample biography of which more than one half is devoted to James's reign as King of England. Uses original authorities accurately, but tends to approach through the medium of recent writings on particular topics. Probably he exaggerates James's abnormalities, and, though he rebuts the idea that James was a fool, he underrates his achievement.

RAIT, Sir ROBERT S. and CAMERON, ANNIE I. *King James's Secret*. Nisbet, 1927. 12*s*. 6*d*.

Based on the Warrender Manuscripts (probably known to earlier historians, but not used for the sake of James's reputation). They show that James made no desperate effort to save his mother in 1587. Yet they make it clear that it was not in James's power to save her.

STAFFORD, HELEN G. *James VI of Scotland and the Throne of England*. New York, 1940.

Based on original documents, some in MSS. A very useful book.

THE SEVENTEENTH CENTURY

MATHEW, DAVID. *Scotland under Charles I*. Eyre & Spottiswoode, 1955. 30*s*.

A book in the new manner. A series of essays by a Roman Catholic who seems to have found the Covenanters more to his taste than the Erastian bishops. An astonishing omission of any consideration of the Act of Revocation, 1625, which had such momentous consequences for Church and State in Scotland. Good use made of material published by the Scottish Clubs, but little used by other writers. Some good vignettes.

DONALDSON, GORDON. *The Making of the Scottish Prayer Book of* 1637. Edinburgh University Press, 1954. 25*s*.

Shows that the Prayer Book should not be called 'Laud's Liturgy' since Laud wanted to introduce the English Prayer

Book as it stood, and it was the King and certain Scottish bishops who insisted on the amendments which were regarded as 'Popish'. But as appears from the citations from Laud's own diaries and papers (see *Recalling the Scottish Covenants*, Hugh Watt, Nelson, 1946) the royal policy in Scotland was part of 'Thorough'. See also *The Story of the Scottish Covenants in Outline* by D. Hay Fleming (Oliphant, Anderson & Ferrier, 1904).

BUCHAN, JOHN. *Montrose*. Nelson, 1928. 10*s*. 6*d*.

A vigorous vindication of Montrose, not only as a soldier of genius, but as a statesman of great wisdom. Based on good evidence including, however, Napier's *Memoirs of Montrose*, 2 vols, 1856, now found to be less reliable than was supposed. See *Challenge to the Highlander*, A. W. W. Ramsay (Murray, 2nd edn., 1936)—six essays contrasting royalist champions, Montrose among them, and their opponents.

HEWISON, J. KING. *The Covenanters*. 2 vols. John Smith, 1908.

A well documented vindication of the Covenanters; but see *Sir George Mackenzie his Life and Times*, Andrew Lang (Longmans, 1909) for a favourable estimate of 'Bloody' Mackenzie.

TAYLER, A. and H. *John Graham of Claverhouse*. Duckworth, 1939.

A eulogy of Montrose, founded upon good evidence, written by two convinced admirers of the Jacobites. They prove the courage and fidelity of their hero.

THE UNION OF THE PARLIAMENTS

MACKINNON, J. *The Union of England and Scotland*. Longmans, 1896.

A narrative chronologically arranged. No index, but full chapter headings. Very good as presenting fully the various arguments used on either side.

DICEY, A. V. and RAIT, Sir ROBERT S. *Thoughts on the Union between England and Scotland*. Macmillan, 1920.

A discussion, topically arranged, of various aspects of the questions by two constitutional historians. A very useful appendix traces the movement towards union down the centuries.

PRYDE, G. S. *The Treaty of Union of Scotland and England of* 1707. Nelson, 1950. 5s.

Short but very good. It contains the text of the treaty and the two supporting treaties dealing with the Churches of Scotland and England. The discussion of the consequences of the Union carries the argument down to the present day. Extremely useful. There are many other books on the Union. Of particular value is G. M. Trevelyan's account in the second volume of his *England under Queen Anne: Ramillies and the Union with Scotland* (Longmans, 1932. 21s.).

THE EIGHTEENTH CENTURY

There is an immense literature on the subject of the Jacobites. Sanford Terry produced *The Jacobites and the Union* and *The Forty-Five* (C.U.P., 1922); each book is a narrative compiled entirely from contemporary authorities. More recently Alistair and Henrietta Tayler have used contemporary sources, among them the Stuart Papers at Windsor, to produce a number of volumes strongly 'Jacobite' in sentiment, but well documented: among them *1715* (Nelson, 1936) and *1745 and After* (Nelson, 1938); the latter is of interest as it includes the narrative (printed for the first time) of O'Sullivan, one of the Irishmen who accompanied Prince Charles. A few representative books of recent date may be noted.

NICHOLAS, DONALD. *The Young Adventurer*. Batchworth, 1949. 8s. 6d.

An extremely fair account by one whose sympathies are with the Jacobites.

HARTMANN, C. H. *The Quest Forlorn*. Heinemann, 1952. 18s.

An essentially 'reasonable' account. Fair, but on the whole rather 'English' in its approach.

FERGUSSON, Sir JAMES, Bt., OF KILKERRAN. *Argyll and the Forty-Five*. Faber, 1951. 21s.

Important as emphasising the importance of the English Navy and of the strength of the anti-Jacobite sentiment in Scotland, with its bastion in Argyll.

27

MEIKLE, H. W. *Scotland and the French Revolution.* J. MacLehose, 1912.

Still the standard authority. Well documented and written with detachment.

MODERN SCOTLAND

During the nineteenth century, the interest of historians of Scotland tended to move towards social and economic history, and some of the essential books are listed in the section devoted to these subjects.

SAUNDERS, L. J. *Scottish Democracy, 1815–1840.* Oliver & Boyd, 1950. 21*s.*

A comprehensive work, founded upon immense research by an author who was interested perhaps in group movement rather than personalities. This volume deals primarily with social and intellectual background, between 1815 and 1840. A second volume was projected, but owing to the author's death, has not appeared.

FLEMING, J. A. *The Church in Scotland.* 2 vols. T. & T. Clark, Vol. 1, *1843–1874,* 1927, 11*s.* 6*d.*; Vol. 2, *1875–1929,* 1933, 14*s.*

Discusses the history of Scotland from the Disruption (1843) to 1929; covers the period during which ecclesiastical affairs played a much bigger part than is now remembered. For the Disruption itself there is a considerable literature, *e.g.*, *Annals of the Disruption* by Thomas Brown (MacNiven and Wallace, new edn. 1893).

MEIKLE, H. W., ed. *Scotland.* Nelson, 1947. 18*s.*

A series of essays by recognised authorities dealing with almost every aspect of the Scotland of the present day. Well illustrated.

GIBB, A. DEWAR. *Scotland Resurgent.* Aeneas Mackay, 1950, 12*s.* 6*d.*

An eloquent appraisal of Scotland's relations with England down the centuries, written from a strongly Nationalist point of view. Those who do not accept all the argument may yet feel there is justice in the assertion that the English point of view has too much prevailed in the writing of British history.

There is considerable 'nationalist' literature, amongst which may be noted:

　　Alexander, MacLehose and Orr, Sir John Boyd. *The Scotland of our Sons*. A. MacLehose, 1937.
　　Walkinshaw, Colin. *The Scots Tragedy*. Routledge, 1935.
　　Thomson, Malcolm G. *Scotland That Distressed Area*. Edinburgh, The Porpoise Press, 1935.

COUPLAND, Sir REGINALD. *Welsh and Scottish Nationalism*, Collins, 1954. 25s.

A balanced book by an expert.

For other books on modern Scotland, see the following sections.

SOCIAL AND ECONOMIC HISTORY

GRANT, I. F. *The Social and Economic Development of Scotland before 1603*. Oliver & Boyd, 1930.

A sober and well documented book of great utility. It is a matter of regret that no second volume ever appeared.

MACKINNON, J. *The Social and Industrial History of Scotland*. 2 vols. Longmans, 1921.

The first volume is rather general, but the second volume is arranged topically. Contains some interesting statistics, though the evidence is not always organised.

FRANKLIN, T. BEDFORD. *A History of Scottish Farming*. Nelson, 1952. 12s. 6d.

Good for the work of the early monastic farmers. Slight for the more recent periods.

HANDLEY, JAMES E. *Scottish Farming in the Eighteenth Century*. Faber, 1953. 25s.

Probably gives too gloomy a picture, and does not lay enough stress upon the improvement visible at the end of the century.

GRAHAM, H. GREY. *The Social Life of Scotland in the Eighteenth Century*. A. & C. Black. 2nd edn., 1900; illustrated edn., 1950. 18s.

Still a standard work, lively and readable; the poverty and squalor which marked the beginning of the century perhaps exaggerated. See also the author's *Scottish Men of Letters in the Eighteenth Century* (1901).

PLANT, M. *The Domestic Life of Scotland in the Eighteenth Century*. Edinburgh University Press, 1952. 25*s*.

An interesting study of all aspects of domestic life, showing that Scotland was not without comforts in the eighteenth century.

HALDANE, A. R. B. *The Drove Roads of Scotland*. Nelson, 1952. 30*s*.

A good book, equipped with an excellent map. Reveals the existence of a cattle trade which was far bigger, and far better organised, than has been generally supposed.

HAMILTON, HENRY. *The Industrial Revolution in Scotland*. O.U.P., 1932.

The standard work. Of great value. Copies are hard to obtain.

FERGUSON, THOMAS. *The Dawn of Scottish Social Welfare*. Nelson, 1948.

A comprehensive history of the development of the care of poverty and sickness in Scotland; detailed from the eighteenth century on. A valuable book.

CAIRNCROSS, A. K., ed. *The Scottish Economy*. C.U.P., 1954. 30*s*.

A statistical account of Scottish life as it has been during the past few decades and as it was in 1954. Extremely useful as a reference book. Well arranged with abundant tables.

HAMILTON, T. *Poor Relief in South Ayrshire*. Oliver & Boyd, 1942. 9*s*. 6*d*.

A brief but extremely useful study of a great question in microcosm, based on the original sources.

MACDONALD, D. J. *Scotland's Shifting Population*. Jackson, 1937.

A well supported study of the effects of industrial concentration, emigration and immigration. Illustrated by effective maps.

SCOTTISH CONSTITUTIONAL HISTORY

CAMERON, JOHN. *Celtic Law*. William Hodge, 1937. 18*s*.

The only book on the subject; necessarily draws much on Irish analogies for its account of Scottish Laws, but uses the Book of Deer and other Scottish evidence.

*RAIT, Sir ROBERT S. *The Parliaments of Scotland.* MacLehose, Jackson, 1924.

Indispensable; the standard book, written by a scholar who knew both the English and the Scottish constitutions. It put the Scottish Parliament in a proper perspective.

COOPER, Lord. *Select Scottish Cases of the Thirteenth Century.* William Hodge, 1944. 15s.

Shows the contribution made to Scottish Law by the Roman Law used by ecclesiastical judges. Along with the views of the writer expressed in his introductions to the *Register of Brieves,* 1946, and *Regiam Majestatem,* 1947 (both Stair Society), and in *The Dark Age of Scottish Legal History,* (Pamphlet) Jackson, 1952, develops the theory that Scots Law was a more definite thing than was supposed, and that the avoidance of the English proliferation of writs was due partly, at least, to an adherence to principles.

HANNAY, ROBERT KERR. *The College of Justice.* William Hodge, 1933. 7s. 6d.

Established the fact that the College of Justice was not a new court founded in 1532 by James V, but was a definition of the old 'Session' itself, at first a function of Parliament, though it had become 'Conciliar' after 1478. Suggests that the new name was given to explain things to the Pope, and justify his grant of a Bull permitting the crown to tax the clergy. In fact the new court was promised only in the Parliament of 1532; the Pope ratified it only in 1535; and only in 1541 was the College of Justice ratified by the Scottish Parliament. Not an easy book to read, but important.

MACKENZIE, W. MACKAY. *The Scottish Burghs.* Oliver & Boyd, 1949. 18s.

A brief and compact history of an institution, important both for the economic and the constitutional history of Scotland. Conclusions based on the story of actual burghs; some modern critics think the net might have been cast wider. A good book.

—— *The Mediaeval Castle in Scotland.* Methuen, 1927.

Traces the development of the Scottish castle from the first motte-and-bailey to the palatial buildings of the seventeenth century. Important for constitution, since the castle represented alike the authority of the feudal baron, and of the crown. The early sheriff was in effect a 'castellan' and many of the burghs arose from settlements about the early castles. See *The Sheriff Court Book of Fife, Introduction and Appendices* by W. Croft Dickinson. S.H.S. 1928.

PAGAN, THEODORA. *The Convention of the Royal Burghs of Scotland.* Glasgow University Press, 1926.

Study of the development and working of a Convention which arose from small beginnings and came to be a sort of economic Parliament. By the beginning of the seventeenth century, the Convention had begun to hold a special meeting at the time and place of the meeting of the Scottish Parliament, of which the burgesses formed a definite estate. (See Mackie and Pryde, *Estate of the Burgesses in the Scots Parliament*, Henderson, St. Andrews, 1923; see also Dr. Pryde's Introduction to *Ayr Burgh Accounts*. S.H.S. 1937).

ECCLESIASTICAL HISTORY

Religion was so much bound up with the history of Scotland that many of the books already noted touch upon Ecclesiastical history. The standard histories are:

CUNNINGHAM, JOHN. *The Church History of Scotland.* 2nd edn. 2 vols. James Thin, Edinburgh, 1882.

A full narrative history by a Principal of St. Mary's College, St. Andrews. Presbyterian, but not provocative or combative.

MACEWEN, A. R. *The History of the Church in Scotland.* 2 vols. Hodder & Stoughton, 1913–18.

A more recent history from a Presbyterian standpoint. Owing to the death of the author concludes with the year 1560. A very good book. Documented.

GRUB, GEORGE. *Ecclesiastical History of Scotland.* 4 vols. Edmonston & Douglas, 1861.

A full and learned history from the point of view of a Scottish Episcopalian. Praised by W. E. Gladstone. Marked by fairness.

BELLESHEIM, ALPHONS. *The History of the Catholic Church in Scotland.* Trans. D. Oswald Hunter Blair. Blackwood, 1887–90.

The work of a very learned German. Hunter Blair's translation has been criticised by Hay Fleming, but it is still the standard history of the Roman Catholic Church in Scotland.

EDUCATION IN SCOTLAND

GRANT, JAMES. *History of the Burgh Schools of Scotland.* Collins, 1876.

Still a recognised standard.

MORGAN, ALEXANDER. *Scottish University Studies.* O.U.P., 1933.

A well-informed study topically arranged.

KNOX, H. M. *Two Hundred and Fifty Years of Scottish Education.* Oliver & Boyd, 1953. 15s.

An admirable summary which takes the narrative from the eighteenth century to the present day.

Among some recent works on particular Universities are:—

CANT, R. G. *The University of St. Andrews.* Oliver & Boyd, 1946. 8s. 6d.

Brief but extremely good. Well documented.

—— *The College of St. Salvator.* Oliver & Boyd, 1950. 15s.

Specialised study of a remarkable College, admirably documented. *cf.* the life of the founder, *The Life and Times of James Kennedy* by Dr. Annie I. Dunlop (see p. 23 *supra*).

DICKINSON, W. CROFT. *Two Students at St. Andrews.* Oliver & Boyd, 1952. 15s.

An illuminating study of student life in the early eighteenth century. For student life at the beginning of the nineteenth century, see *Duncan Dewar* by Sir Peter Scott Lang (Jackson, Wylie, 1926).

SCOTT, W. R. *Adam Smith as Student and Professor.* Jackson, 1937. 30s.

Sheds valuable light not only on the development of Smith's ideas, but on his administrative work in a University. Very well documented.

MACKIE, J. D. *The University of Glasgow.* Jackson, 1954. 15*s.*

Sets the development of the University of Glasgow over five hundred years against the background of Scottish History.

TURNER, A. LOGAN. *History of the University of Edinburgh,* 1833–1933. Oliver & Boyd, 1933. 10*s.*

An excellent and full work, topically arranged, with good biographical notes. Continues the history from where it was left in the standard work on the subject *The Story of the University of Edinburgh during its First Three Hundred Years* by Sir Alexander Grant, 2 vols. (Longmans, 1884).

THE HIGHLANDS

Out of many books, the following may be selected:—

GREGORY, DONALD. *The History of the Western Highlands and Islands.* 2nd edn. Hamilton, Adams, 1881.

The work of an author who made good use of the Gaelic sources. Never superseded.

KELTIE, J. S. *A History of the Scottish Highlands, Highland Clans, and Highland Regiments.* 2 vols. Fullarton, 1879.

Well illustrated. Despite its perhaps unpromising title, a great repository of information not easily obtainable elsewhere.

INNES, Sir THOMAS OF LEARNEY. *The Tartans of the Clans and Families of Scotland.* rev. edn. W. & A. K. Johnston, 1950. 18*s.*

Contains, besides reproductions of Clan tartans and notes on each Clan, an essay by the present Lyon King of Arms upon the origin and nature of the Scottish Clans.

Clan Histories. W. & A. K. Johnston, 1952–55. Each 5*s.*

Brief but well illustrated histories of various clans by authors of repute. The following are available:—

The Clan Cameron; The Clan Campbell; The Clan Donald; The Clan Fraser of Lovat; The Clan Gordon; The Clan Grant; The Clan MacGregor; The Clan Mackay; The Clan Mackenzie; The Clan Maclean; The Clan Macleod; The Clan Munro; The Robertsons; The Stewarts.

Many other Clan Histories, some on a very large scale, have been published.

SCOTLAND AND THE EMPIRE

The great part played by Scotsmen in the development of the British Empire is written all over the histories of the various dominions and colonies. See for example, the *Cambridge History of the British Empire*. Three special books may be mentioned:—

INSH, GEORGE PRATT. *Scottish Colonial Schemes*. MacLehose, Jackson, 1922.

Describes the attempts of the Scots to found colonies in Nova Scotia, Cape Breton and Carolina during the seventeenth century.

—— *The Company of Scotland*. Scribner, 1932.

A lively account of the Scottish attempt to found a colony at Darien, by an author who had made a full study of the original documents (in part published in his *Darien Shipping Papers*. S.H.S. 1924).

GIBB, A. DEWAR. *Scottish Empire*. A. MacLehose, 1937.

A succinct, but comprehensive account of the great part played by Scotsmen in developing the Empire in Canada, Africa, India, Australia, New Zealand and the Pacific.

SCOTTISH ART

(Only a few recent books are mentioned)

FINLAY, IAN. *Art in Scotland*. O.U.P., 1948.

A study setting the history of Scottish art into the background of political and social developments.

CURSITER, STANLEY. *Scottish Art*. Harrap, 1949.

A well produced book with splendid illustrations by a recognized authority on Scottish painting.

SMART, ALASTAIR. *The Life and Art of Allan Ramsay*. Routledge, 1952. 30s.

A careful and well illustrated study of a Scottish painter whose work (perhaps because it was followed by that of Raeburn) has only recently been given the appreciation it deserves.

GORDON, T. CROUTHER. *David Allan*. R. Cunningham, Alva, 1951. 30*s*.

A well illustrated account of an artist who in some ways forestalled Wilkie,—' The Scottish Hogarth'.

MACGIBBON, D. and ROSS T. *The Castellated and Domestic Architecture of Scotland from the Twelfth to the Eighteenth Century*. 5 vols. Douglas, 1887–92.

—— *The Ecclesiastical Architecture of Scotland from the Earliest Times to the Seventeenth Century*. 3 vols. Douglas, 1896–7.

The standard works.

HANNAH, I. C. *The Story of Scotland in Stone*. Oliver & Boyd, 1934.

A brief history of the development of Scottish architecture up to the period of the Renaissance. Illustrated; and explained to the layman.

STIRLING-MAXWELL, Sir JOHN. *Shrines and Homes of Scotland*. A. MacLehose and W. & R. Chambers, 1937.

A beautifully illustrated book on the churches, castles and houses of Scotland by a great humanist.

SCOTTISH LITERATURE

Generally speaking the best sources of information upon Scottish literature are to be found in the good editions of the Scottish Text Society.

Here literature can be considered only in so far as it bears upon Scottish history. The works of Scott and Galt, for example, are very valuable for the eighteenth century and the early nineteenth. There are many editions of Scott's works, but no single edition of the works of Galt, though *The Works of John Galt*, ed. T. S. Meldrum and William Roughead (Edinburgh, John Grant, 1936, 10 vols., 57*s*. 6*d*. the set) contains some of the best known books beautifully printed with illustrations by C. E. Brock. There are many editions of the works of Burns. A handsome omnibus edition is *The Complete Writings of Robert Burns*, ed. F. H. Allen, 10 vols. (Waverley Book Company, 1927). *The Poetry of Robert*

Burns is found in the Centenary Edition ed. Henley & Henderson; 4 vols. (Jack: Edinburgh, 1896–97). The letters are best studied in:

The Letters of Robert Burns, ed. J. de Lancey Ferguson, 2 vols. O.U.P., 1931. 63*s*.

A few special books are mentioned here:—

HENDERSON, T. F. *Scottish Vernacular Literature: A Succinct History*. Edinburgh, John Grant, 1910.

The most useful handbook.

MILLAR, J. H. *A Literary History of Scotland*. T. Fisher Unwin, 1903.

A comprehensive account, marked by the writer's predilections, and without an index. Vigorous and well informed.

—— *Scottish Prose of the Seventeenth and Eighteenth Centuries*. J. MacLehose, 1912.

Contains samples from well-known authors.

GRAHAM, H. GREY. *Scottish Men of Letters in the Eighteenth Century*. A. & C. Black, 1901.

A recognised standard.

TODD, G. EYRE, ed. *The Abbotsford Series of Scottish Poets*. 7 vols. Sands & Co.

A convenient collection of Scottish poetry from the Middle Ages to the eighteenth century. Well informed introductions. Not very critical.

SCOTT, Sir WALTER. *The Minstrelsy of the Scottish Border*, ed. T. F. Henderson. 4 vols. Oliver & Boyd, 1932.

Much the best edition.

Of late, a revival of Scottish vernacular poetry has produced many books. Samples of the recent poetry may be found in:—

New Scots Poetry. A selection of short poems from the Festival of Britain Scots Poetry Competition arranged by the Scottish Committee of the Arts Council of Great Britain. Serif Books, Edinburgh, 1952.

INDEX OF AUTHORS AND EDITORS

www.ingramcontent.com/pod-product-compliance
Ingram Content Group UK Ltd.
Pitfield, Milton Keynes, MK11 3LW, UK
UKHW020449010325
455719UK00015B/489